Desiderium

L. J. Ward

BookLeaf Publishing

Presentation by *BookLeaf Publishing*

Web: www.bookleafpub.com

E-mail: info@bookleafpub.com

ISBN: 978-93-5744-965-6

First edition 2022

DEDICATION

To those in my life I thought I loved, and one I really did.

ACKNOWLEDGEMENT

To my family—thank you for challenging me and believing in my abilities.

To the one who revealed to me long ago that much of my poetry is underscored by hope—you knew about me what I did not.

To my senior school English teachers—I would not be writing today, in quite this way, without you.

And to my best friend, Kitty—thank you for agonising over and caring for my words in the same way I do.

PREFACE

Love is a very tricky thing.

For a moment it can make you feel like you have everything figured out, and all too soon it can explode into a million little butterflies, all of them flying prettily away from you forever. I am young, but I have felt too much to possibly fit in my small body, and that is what poetry is for—to lighten the pressing load on your heart and make it that much easier to show someone how you feel, or just walk a couple short steps without completely falling apart.

gardens /

I

For the millionth time,
You, you inconsiderate sprite,
Have trampled my daisies.
Oh, look how you tear the roots of the daffodils from their beds of soil and scamper away with them.
The roses whimper at your departure,
The bluebells sink as you blow raspberries behind you,
The apples on the trees go brown with one word from your coquettish lips.
Why don't you just uproot the whole garden?

II

I am a bed of roses
And you pluck from my canopy of soft blooms with a rough hand that swears it means well.
You decorate your photo frames with my nymphet buds and wreath your neck with my crimson petals in attempts to increase your value.

Watch how incessantly you rip the stringy stems
from their roots
For one day there will be none left—
And you will feel yourself slowly begin to
wither away.
And I will blame myself, saying,
"Hark!
Look how his skin yellows and his eyes sadden.
His hair greys and loses its body, his form limp
and his lips sucked dry. I should have warned
him."
But blaming myself is unfair, you see.

(2017)

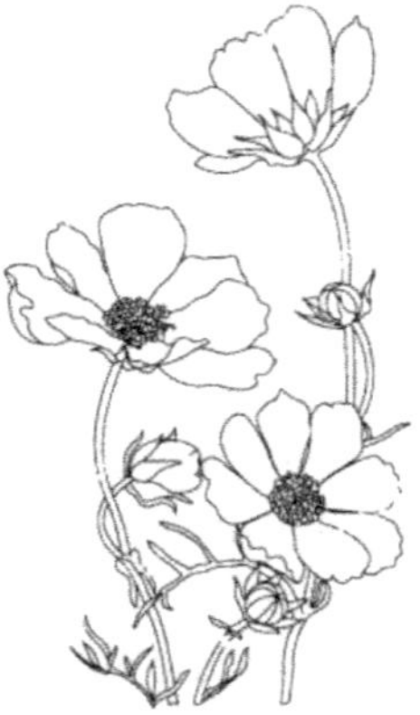

the ice prince /

My first love built me up like an ice castle; he
enjoyed sculpting it, perfecting it.
I expected it to last.
To stand sturdy, strong, magical in every way.
But when summer reached its hottest point the
ice castle began to melt.
He was infuriated. And instead of trying to mend
it, repair it, he decided to break pieces from it,
and threw them so far I couldn't even see where
they landed.
He kicked the foundations of the castle,
dejected.
He ran away, hoping no one saw.
And he left me inside, bloodied with the shards
of an icicle chandelier.

(2017)

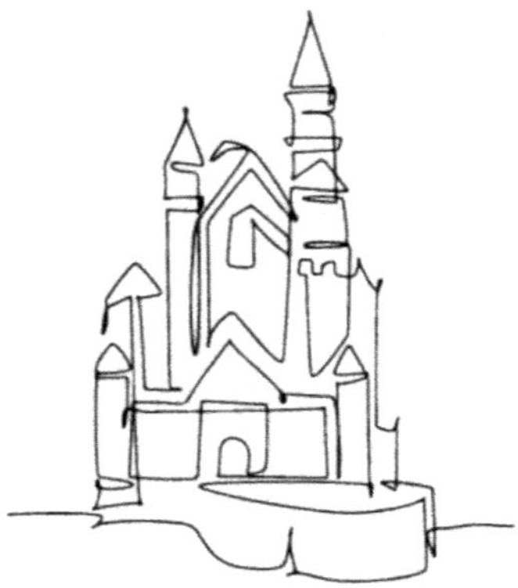

beanstalks /

I stood by the moulting birch tree,
Looking at its trunk,
And the first thing I wondered
Was whether you'd find it climbable.
Would your long fingers not be able
To find a spot to grip
Without a layer of bark pulling away
And landing you on the grass
Or am I underestimating your expertise in
climbing trees?
Or maybe you wouldn't think twice
About climbing this tree;
Maybe you'd go for the smoother one
Across the road
I don't really know your taste in trees
These days
I can't remember
All I really knew
Were the ones you conquered in December

(2017)

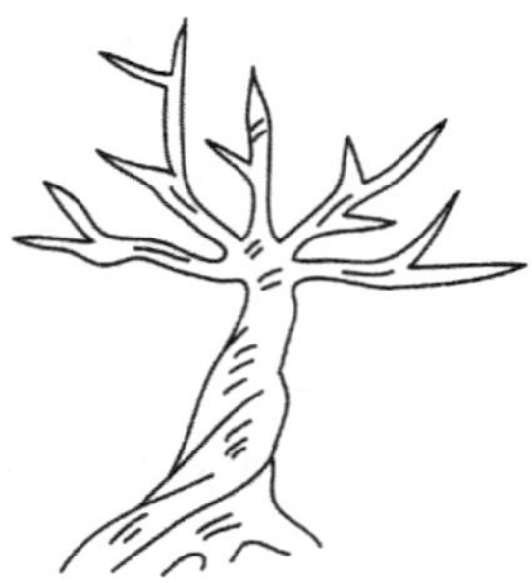

summer /

Summer feels different this time around. As all summers before you did, as all summers to come will. I hesitate to admit I often catch myself expecting that one summer when you were here to reincarnate itself, to return with the burning of the sun.

I feel the heat rising, and my muscle memory almost expects you to not be too far away.

That summer, that Christmas, a million twinkling lights shone within me—nerve endings dancing with an exuberance never felt before and never felt again. You were this entity of possibility and constant excitement, something my body, mind and soul devoured quickly.

I am ashamed to admit that I miss that summer, even though autumn quickly sliced its heart open, and exiled it. I adored watching you climb trees, feeling my heart swell with your every blue-eyed wonder. Listening to you whisper as I lay in your arms beneath that tree—I have not since revisited it.

To revisit it would be to confront the reality that that summer will never come again, I will never kiss you under that tree again—not at all—you will never graze your arms climbing said tree again.

Closure is a fantasy, and December sticks to me like sweat.

(2018)

where are you? /

Where are you?
Look at the sky.
Isn't it beautiful, dear?
It's the grandest shade of ultraviolet,
I like it this way.
It's nice,
You say.
Where did you go?
Did you notice the emerald leaves
Coming in on the angophora trees,
My love?
They're quite green today.
I hadn't noticed,
You say.

Where are you going?
Did you see I wore those satin hair ribbons you like,
Sweetheart?
The ones you chose the other day.
Ah,
You say.
Your eyes are somewhere far away.

(2019)

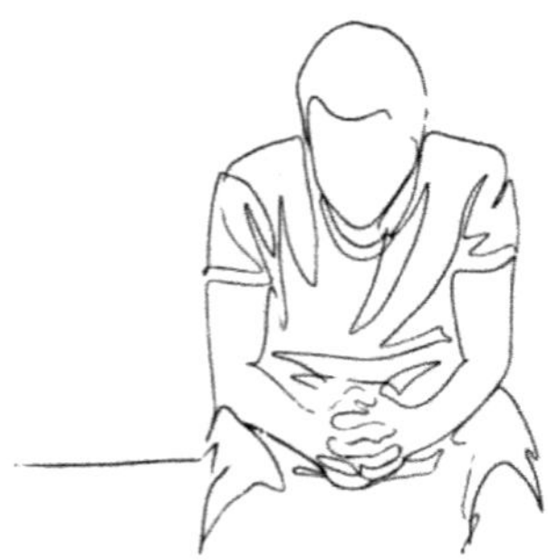

slumber /

Unlike he,
You will always sleep in my heart like a dormant dream,
A heart that is content and relieved that not all men intend to take it and dissect it for fun.

He liked playing with it in his hands
Like a piece of meat he could devour at any moment
He preferred it rare, pulsating with a passion he could never reciprocate
But you touched my heart with feathery hands
Though stronger than his they were
And I promise you
No one will speak ill of you for as long as I live
Because even though your words were rough
You taught me that a man can be soft

(2018)

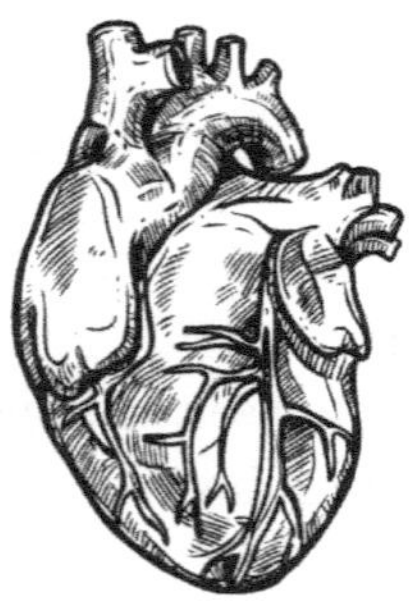

before a breath /

He is busy.
He thinks of train times and lengthy formulas.
I think of Keats, and punctuate stanzas
With his eyes dancing in my skull.
He is tired.
Spare moments make his bed for a microsleep,
During the walk from the sheets to the shower.
I clutch my notebook tightly,
Breakages and splinters between my fingertips.
He is far away.
He speaks of chariots and other things
He's never really known.
I look up and marvel at his ever-present grin—
He is musing of old but not forgotten lore.
I am unstoppable.
My hands grip the chair in front of me;
Tangible, real.
"We" is a placebo.
He is consumed.
He dreams of a life pulled tight,
Permanent stitches.
I chase dandelion fluff and grasp it with my
fingers,
Only for it to slip away once again.

(2018)

settling /

I am infinitely wiser than I was when I last held your hand,
But your pressure on my lungs is ever as hard.
It is not you,
It is routine.
It is loneliness,
It is frustration,
It is me at eighteen.
It is you and me everyday,
It is an understanding either way,
It is two individuals who can't stand to be alone
When I sit silently on the phone on your way home
It is not me,
It is not you,
It is settling for the other cause that's all we can do.
And I wonder what will happen when someone threatens to break these habits
When now, there's no other way I would have it
Who will she be?
Who will he?
What will it take to sever you
And me?

(2019)

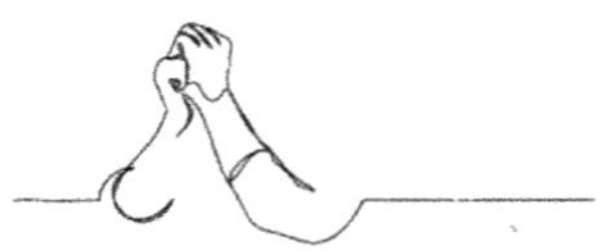

ego /

You touch me and a shiver runs down my spine.
Don’t flatter yourself, your hands are just
cold

(2019)

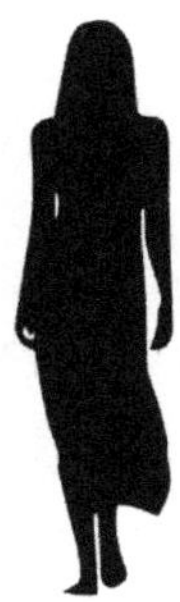

fanfare /

I've had a taste of triumph.

The brassy fanfare welcomes me with a parade of ornamented sirens, and the palace builds around me, yielding the promise of luxury and comfort.

The ladies-in-waiting offer me the most expensive gowns and jewels but all I want is to rest my head and indulge in my dreams of dented knights with heavy armour.

(unknown)

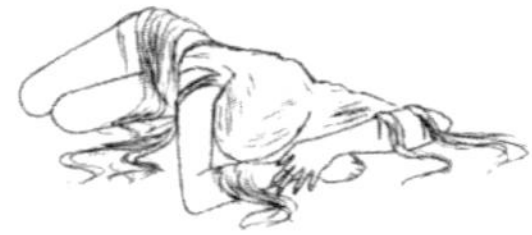

hibernation /

And I will wait
For the second coming of love
Like Christians for their Messiah
Hibernating in this dark, cold tomb
You have made for me
That I have closed by rolling the stone over the opening.
I lay in silken robes that cover my skin
Like the stillest of waters
Only rippling over my bare body
When I move to sit up from my slumber
When I hear clearly
So very clearly
His voice calling me out from hiding
Saying,
It is safe to emerge, my love,
You have waited with grace and patience
And I will rise, and go to him.

(2018)

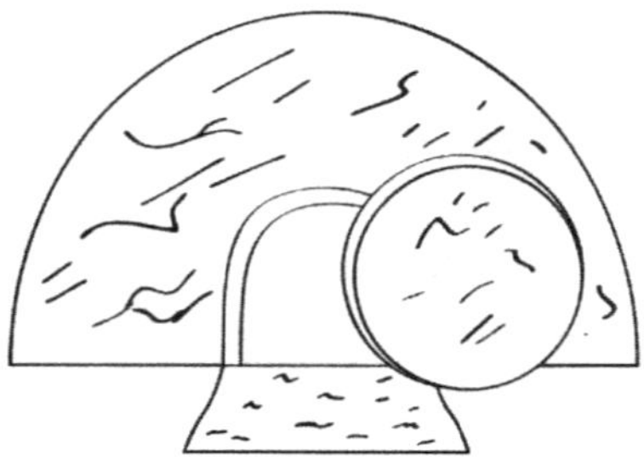

morendo /

I imagined you going out with a bang.
With a blow to the chest, an ache on the bus,
regret in my throat and a peak in my lust.
I prospected that the end of us would have been
a year earlier, or decades later. When you got
engaged, or when I turned the page. After an
attempted casual relationship where our bodies
met once again, and I decided you weren't for
me, in any format.
But you fizzled out like popping candy losing its
enthusiasm on my tongue, and I didn't even see
your figure fade out of sight.

(2019)

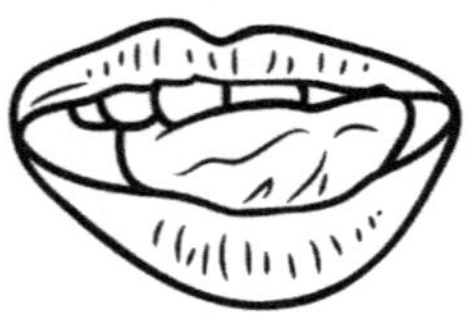

generous /

With the heart of a lion
As broad as the Pacific Ocean
A roar heard over the sea
But delicate in his words,
With his eyes,
You will never meet another like
He

(2019)

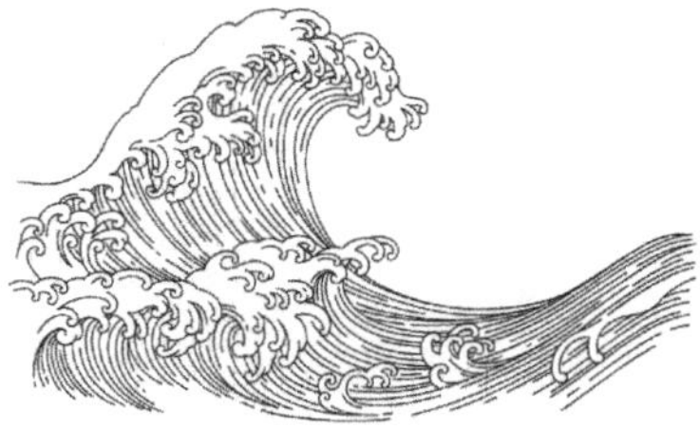

a real man /

This one outsmarted the others.
He continues to outsmart them as I type.
He is a balanced scale, never frail, always
willing.
He asks for my hand before I even begin to
yearn for his, while the others walked far ahead
of me and didn't understand what it meant for
me, to have my hand held.
His heavy arms hold me carefully, regarding me
simultaneously brand new china and
glued-together glass.
He chased me like a curious little boy,
Sprinting after a butterfly, and when he
whispers, "perfect", I softly wonder why.
Emotionally aware, and literate of heart, he crept
in right under my nose—
my lucky bullseye dart.

(2019)

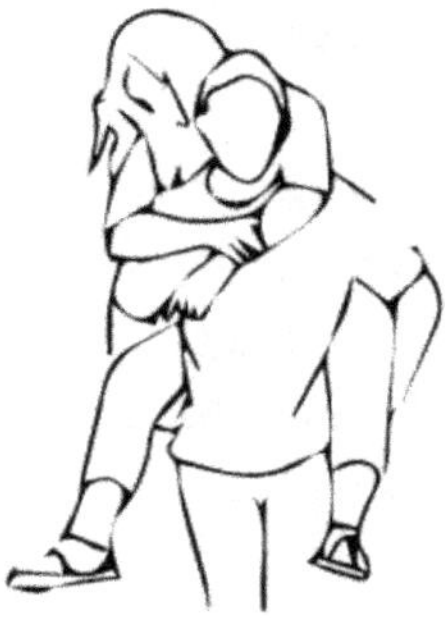

yin & yang /

Moments with you
Where forever doesn't sound so bad
Where everything is burgundy
And I feel a safe kind of mad
Where nobody can tell us
Enough is enough
And red lights are even
Rooting for love

When your eyes are unpredictable
Like the forest when the sun
Makes fractals through the leaves
Or the deepest brown wood
On the forest floor
Keeping up the trees

You're my little sun
And I am your moon
Like yin and yang—
But I speak too soon:
In our kisses I feel
We are but the same
Same currents in our bodies
And your name in my name

(2020)

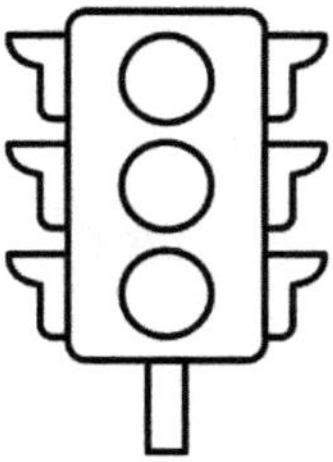

cold rock /

I hold onto you with both hands,
All at once.
You drive quietly, and I sink further into the passenger seat.
You laugh and I feel at home in the world, my face in your neck, your hand on my waist.
Finally, a soul that tethers to my own with a certainty I've never known, and perhaps will never know again.

(2020)

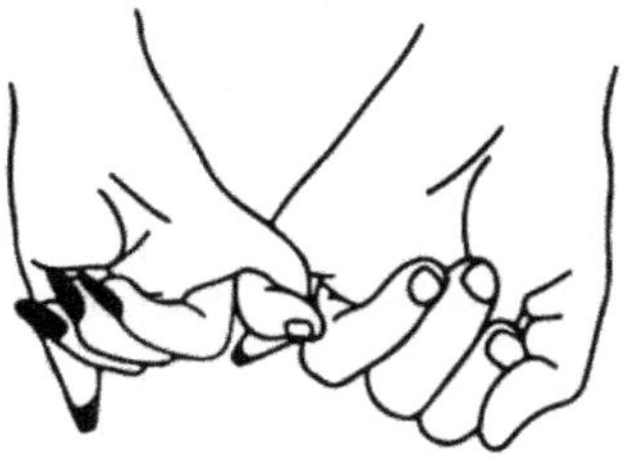

not lucky, but blessed /

You tiptoed into my life through my periphery:
In chaotic nights and God's cleverest trickery
You waited for me to come to the table
Before you started eating
And as soon as I was able
I returned with what you needed

We've seen the dark, it's true;
I have seen you as alight as coarse I have seen you.
And I have cried
And I have wondered what you really expected me to do.
There have been empty gym sets
And closed doors
And the withholding of kisses
And "what was that for"s
But through it all I find you
Underneath all the layers
Underneath the quiet
Between the never-sayers

In unspoken words
In lovingly wandering eyes
In chuckles and childish racing
And insistent "I'm fine"s
I feel you as vividly as I feel myself
And although you are different
You're closer than anyone else
And you must know just how singular I find
you.

(2021)

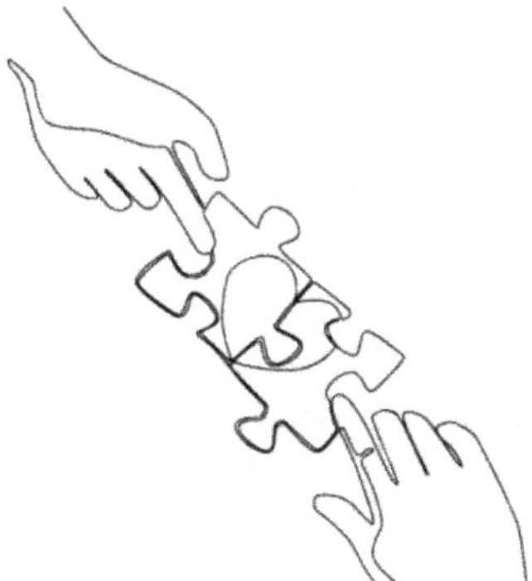

anti-gravity /

When resistance floods your space
Wring your hands of it, my love
Filter your thoughts through me
For I only live for you

When they place a hot stone in your hands and say,
Prove your love with your pain
My tears will cool your palms
Each and everyday

If you ever feel as if
My love burdens your soul
Exorcise it
Burn it to charcoal
I want to be your anti-gravity
Don't let me weigh you down
I want you to fly
I can watch from the ground

(2021)

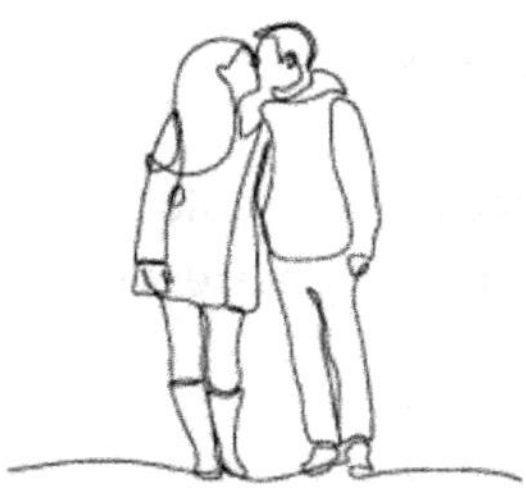

2 minutes /

I watch you,
Seconds apart but my jumper-clad skin feels naked
The hairs stand up demanding warmth
In a twenty-eight-degree room.
I stare at the curve of your arm, your chin rested on the inside of your hand.

"Give me a minute,"
He says,
And it's perfectly reasonable
But when you are this perfect how could I ever be reasonable?

Come back
By my side
For 6 months all I've done is lied
To them
And I swear for a week there
I breathed less than I cried
But again

Like the sun goes down and the moon hides away

Night comes and goes but it’s worth a glimpse of day
And every valley we fall into from the sky
Lets us discover the light fifty-thousand times
I fall in love
From just seconds away
Because I know when you settle
You always stay

(2021)

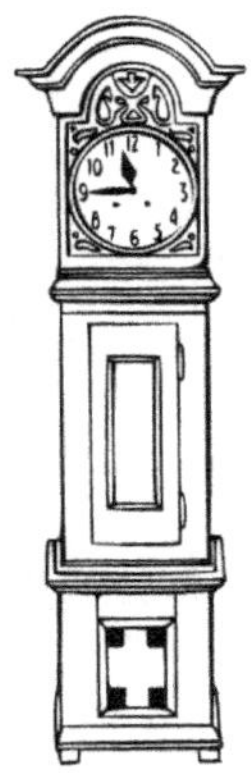

restraint /

And she knew he loved her from his restraint—
His patterns of explosion, and decrescendo, and
climax and composure.
He withheld and he sat still, breathed like his
mind were an ocean of simple serenity; stagnant,
Satisfied,
P e r f e c t

And she loved him because of the lion that
roared within him—
Insatiable, untameable, uncontainable.
A passionate animal with limbs made for
destruction
But a capability for the gentlest touch
And he ebbed and flowed like a song,
His energy following her movement.

But one day he was so collected
So still and needless,
Seemingly self-regulating and self-absorbed
That she began to feel nothing from him;
No vibrations,
No ravening murmurs or hummingbird
heartbeats
No silent understandings

Or cheap kisses

And all of a sudden everything cost
And the animal was gone
And she felt the world within him die away
Like a lion put to sleep

(2021)

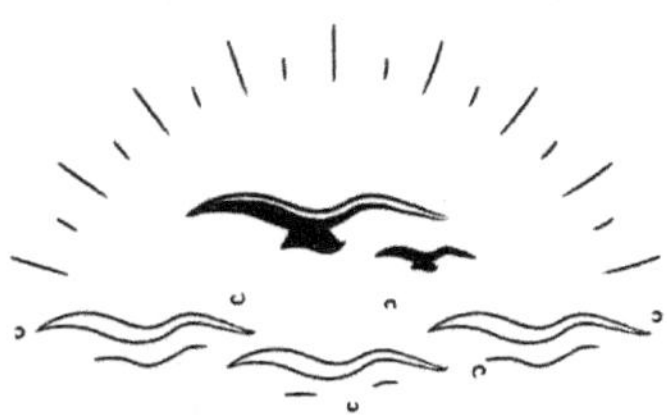

the steward /

The chandelier you speak of;
You curated her from scattered crystals.
She was powerless,
A mess of beads and full of empty missiles.
She was always beautiful,
But she was misled,
Dropped mid-air,
An heirloom they couldn't claim,
For she belonged hung from the ceiling of a
mansion none could afford to upkeep.
And so, the mansion sat,
Cobwebbed and dark,
Until you.

You stepped up with your boots on the marble
floor
With dirty, determined hands
And c r y s t a l   v i s i o n s
For what the place could be.
The centrepiece hangs, now,
Proudly,
In the sparkling drawing room.
Because of you.

God gave me you;

A man with the Heart of Jesus,
Hard, gentle hands and open, always open,
sturdy, soft arms—
Ready to catch me.
The thought of you
Is accompanied with echoes of security, passion,
longing
And above all
Acceptance
For the woman I am, the woman I was and the
woman I am still yet to be.
Forgive me for my impatiences,
My past bitterness and misunderstanding;
I try every day to love you with the purest of
intentions
But I have been trained to always be on the
lookout for cracks in visages
Empty promises
And fools with shockingly handsome faces.
And handsome you are.
I am Watson
And words must always be validated with proof,
For any hedonistic fool can say forever,
And one did.

I see you as a man.
And what keeps you from me
In my stagnant darkness

I can never envision as powerful enough to
override your mind
I’ve thought and overthought,
Some countless times
I have protested and I've
Believe me; I’ve tried

When you say you have obligations,
I can’t fathom them.
For I know you love me so,
And so where could you possibly have to go?
Where could you possibly have to be?
Where are you going?
Where have you been?
And before I know it,
Where have you gone?

All I see is the man I fell in love with
My chest swells when I remember him
When I think of you
How you got things done
Your consistency
Your reliability
Thoughtfulness
And independence
But I only see what you let me see
And so I wonder,
And I am Watson every time.

The brim of this hat is wide
I am sheltered
I do not know the ins and outs of your misery
And its test tube parents
I only know of my misery
And my very strict list of instructions

But I see you come in every day,
However long it is for.
I see you sweep the floors and polish the silver
and clean the mirrors with elbow grease until
they shine you back at you
And I wonder when you'll recognise yourself
again.

I see you dust the chandelier delicately
And I know she loves you from the way she
twinkles when you pass under her
In the centre of the drawing room
And I know she waits patiently for you every
day
Because even though you are gone so much
When you finally arrive, you prove worth
awaiting
Listen to her clink happily with the wind when
you open the windows to let her breathe.

(2021)

www.ingramcontent.com/pod-product-compliance
Lightning Source LLC
Chambersburg PA
CBHW051739130826
49812CB00033B/924
9789357449656